How to be an Aztec Warrior

Written by
Fiona Macdonald

Illustrated by
Dave Antram
Mark Bergin

BOOK HOUSE

Fiona Macdonald studied History at Cambridge University and at the University of East Anglia. She has taught in schools and adult education, and is the author of numerous books for children on historical topics.

Mark Bergin studied at Eastbourne College of Art and has specialised in historical reconstructions, aviation and maritime subjects for over 20 years. He lives in Bexhill-on-Sea with his wife and three children.

Series created and designed by **David Salariya**
Editor **Penny Clarke**
Fact Consultant **Dr Tim Laughton**
Lecturer in pre-Columbian culture at the University of Essex

Published in Great Britain in 2005 by
Book House, an imprint of
The Salariya Book Company Ltd
25 Marlborough Place, Brighton BN1 1UB

Please visit the Salariya Book Company at:
www.salariya.com

ISBN 1-904642-99-3

A catalogue record for this book is available from the British Library.
Printed and bound in China.
The Salariya Book Company operates an environmentally friendly policy wherever possible.

Visit our website at **www.book-house.co.uk**
for free electronic versions of:
You wouldn't want to be an Egyptian Mummy!
You wouldn't want to be a Roman Gladiator!
Avoid joining Shackleton's Polar Expedition!
Avoid sailing on a 19th-century Whaling Ship!

Photographic credits
t=top b=bottom c=centre l=left r=right

Ancient Art and Architecture Collection: 25b
The Art Archive / Bodleian Library Oxford / The Bodleian Library: 18
The Art Archive / Mexican National Library / Mireille Vautier: 8
The Art Archive / Museo del Templo Mayor Mexico / Dagli Orti: 21
The Art Archive / Museo Etnografico Pigorini Rome / Dagli Orti: 13,
The Art Archive / Museum für Völkerkunde Vienna / Dagli Orti: 12

The Art Archive / National Anthropological Museum Mexico / Dagli Orti: 11, 15, 23, 25t
The Art Archive / National Archives Mexico / Mireille Vautier: 17, 29

Every effort has been made to trace copyright holders. The Salariya Book Company apologises for any unintentional omissions and would be pleased, in such cases, to add an acknowledgement in future editions.

Warrior Required

How would you like to join the team that defends your people and your homeland?

The Aztec army has vacancies for strong young soldiers who are keen to seek adventure, win fame and praise for their bravery, and please the Aztec gods.

Your main duties will include:

- Defending your city against invaders.

- Conquering new territory.

- Controlling conquered peoples and collecting tribute from them.

- Most importantly of all, taking captives to sacrifice to the gods.

How to join? Hurry to the main square of your city when you hear the beat of the big war-drum.

(An interest in the Aztec empire would be a great advantage.)

Contents

What you should know

Be prepared for a journey back in time – to the years between AD 1300 and 1500. That's when the Aztecs were most powerful. From their capital city, Tenochtitlán (now known as Mexico City), they ruled a large empire in Mesoamerica, home to many different peoples. You'll find it's a harsh environment and full of contrasts. There are high mountains, active volcanoes, dry deserts and tropical rainforests. It's hot and dusty during the day, but bitterly cold at night. There are spiders, snakes, eagles and jaguars. You'll see maize-fields on mountain slopes, wild cacao trees that grow beans to make chocolate, and lakeside 'floating gardens', where Aztec farmers grow chillis, peppers and tomatoes.

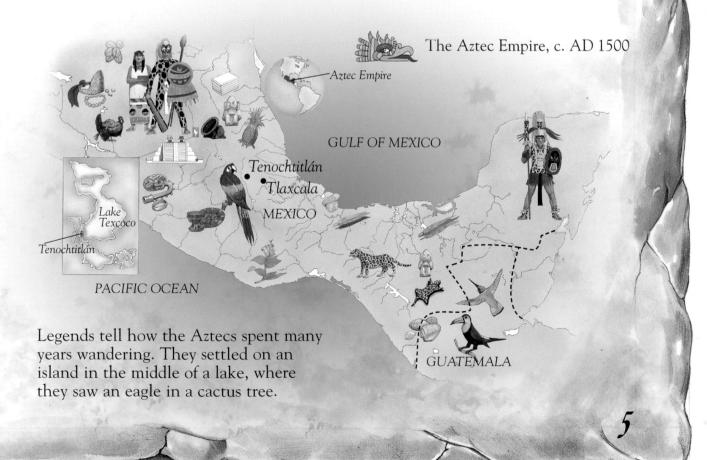

The Aztec Empire, c. AD 1500

Aztec Empire

GULF OF MEXICO

Tenochtitlán
Tlaxcala
MEXICO

Lake Texcoco

Tenochtitlán

PACIFIC OCEAN

GUATEMALA

Legends tell how the Aztecs spent many years wandering. They settled on an island in the middle of a lake, where they saw an eagle in a cactus tree.

Is yours the right family?

Like all other Aztecs, you depend on your family for your place in society. Only nobles are officers. Most soldiers come from ordinary families. So, like them, you'll have very few possessions and your life will be hard. You'll have grown up seeing your mother always busy – cooking, cleaning, weaving and caring for your baby brothers and sisters. In his workshop or fields your father has taught you the skills you'll need to make a living.

▼ You'll live in a mud-brick house, with one room and a grass roof. A round granary, to store maize, is in the courtyard outside.

Granary

Turkeys for food

Weaving

Foot plough for digging fields

Long cotton cloak

Fan

Noble privileges

◄ If you're from a noble family, then your life will be comfortable, although you'll have army duties to carry out in return. You'll have a big house, richly embroidered clothes, feather fans, gold jewellery, leather sandals and lots of food. Slaves and servants will look after you and run your home.

Tlatoani
(emperor)

Cihuacoatl
(deputy ruler)

Priest

Government
official

Noble warrior

Farmer

Thatch

Making
tortillas

Mud-brick
walls

Aztec society

▲ Aztec society is very unequal. The most powerful person is the Tlatoani (emperor). He lives with his family in a huge palace in Tenochtitlán. He is helped by a male deputy called 'Cihuacoatl' (Snake Woman) and hundreds of government officials. He is also advised by nobles who help lead the army. Priests are very powerful. They study the stars, keep records and perform sacrifices in the temples. You are from a poor family, so your wife will carry your children on her back.

Cloak made
of rough
cactus fibre

Bare
feet

Parents and children

▶ You may be a young adult, but you'll still live with your parents. A match-maker will chose your bride for you. If you both have children, you'll have to be strict with them, like other Aztec parents, so they'll grow up respectful and obedient. But as a poor family, your wife will have to look after you all.

Are you loyal to your clan?

Every Aztec, including you, belongs to a *calpulli*. This is a clan or large family group descended from the same ancestor. You'll have to obey calpulli leaders. They're in charge of law and order in your neighbourhood, and organise welfare schemes. Calpullis also run schools for Aztec boys, and teach them to fight. If you want to be a warrior, your calpulli will help train you.

Calpullis

Calpullis control all the land in a neighbourhood. If a farmer refuses to work his fields, or a craftsman to mend his workshop, the calpulli can take it away and give it to someone else.

State taxes

To pay for government – and the empire's armies – all Aztec farmers, craftworkers and traders pay taxes to the emperor.

Don't try to cheat me, or I'll complain to the government.

Stop worrying! I'm your friend! We belong to the same clan.

Is poverty your fate?

◄ The Aztecs believe that some people are fated by the gods to be criminals, or to lead poor, unhappy lives. The goddess Coatlicue, shown in this Aztec codex drawing (see page 10), was believed to bring slavery, poverty and death.

Regular collections

Aztecs give a share of their goods or crops to government officials, who collect them from calpullis every twenty days.

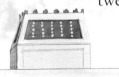

Law and order

Aztec laws are strict. They aim to frighten people into good behaviour. And Aztec punishments are swift, savage and severe. If you are found guilty of robbery, witchcraft, treason, adultery or being drunk in public, you could be executed.

▲ Suspected criminals are brought before a judge.

▶ While waiting for the judge, suspects are locked in a wooden cage.

For a first offence criminals are pardoned or their house might be knocked down. For a second offence there is no mercy. They are strangled (above) or clubbed (right) to death.

◀ Aztec rulers also use bribes and rewards to help make people obey them. They offer gifts of gold to make friends with neighbouring rulers. They give brightly coloured cloaks to soldiers who take captives in battle.

Which school did you go to?

As you know, all Aztec boys go to school – but not all of them are taught to be warriors. When each boy is about fifteen his parents have a choice. Should they send their son to a *calmecac* (temple school) run by priests, or to a *tepochcalli* (house of young men) run by leaders of the local calpulli? Their choice will shape their son's future. Which school did you go to?

▼ At a temple school priests and scribes will have taught you to read and write, as well as how to use three calendars based on holy tradition, the Sun and the planet Venus.

The books you'll use

▼ Aztec books (called 'codices') are made of long strips of fig-bark paper, folded to make pages. The picture-writing is arranged zig-zag across each page, from right to left then left to right, and from the top to the bottom.

Emperor · Sun god

Sketch the outlines in black, then add the colours with your brush.

▲ Scribes wrote using *glyphs* (picture symbols). Some showed items in miniature; others represented ideas. Each had its own sound. The glyphs could be combined, like letters, to spell long words.

Learning to be a warrior

But if, like most Aztec boys, you went to a 'house of young men', you'll know nothing about reading or writing. Instead, you'll have been taught how to repair buildings, cut firewood, dig drainage ditches and work on calpulli farms. You'll have spent your free time with friends, singing and dancing. There are restrictions on spending time with women during training. Most important of all, experienced warriors will have taught you to handle weapons and fight. They will also have taught you to be brave and encouraged you to feel pride.

▶ Two pages of glyphs (picture-writing) from the Codex Mendoza, written by Aztec scribes in the 16th century AD. They show Aztec headdresses, clothing, jewellery, blankets, feather-trimmed shields and army officers' uniforms.

Can you handle weapons?

Every man has to have his own weapons. So are yours ready? Have you got a bow and plenty of arrows, a stone-tipped spear and a sling for hurling pebbles? Do you have a *macquauitl* – a strong wooden sword tipped with razor-sharp blades of obsidian (volcanic glass)? And don't forget your *atlatl* (spear-thrower) to launch plenty of javelins and poison-tipped darts.

▶ This feather shield is decorated with an *auitzotl*, a magic water creature. Priests say it kills people and sends their souls to the skies.

For extra protection

As well as weapons, you'll need a shield. It could even give you super-natural protection if it's decorated with a magic design.

Making a shield

Cut a wide strip of bark from a tree.

Soften it in lime and water.

Use a stone hammer to flatten it.

Clean and sort the feathers.

Cut shield; strengthen with wood.

Glue the feathers on the shield.

Uniforms and emblems

▲ How will you recognise your comrades in battle? Ordinary soldiers (left) wear padded cotton armour, soaked in salt water to make it strong. Top warriors (middle) wear jaguar suits. Army commanders (right) have huge flags or emblems strapped to their backs.

Stronger arms

▶ Wooden *atlatl* (spear-thrower). You'll use this in battle or out hunting to help you throw darts and spears further and faster. Hold the looped end in one hand and fix the spear or dart to the other. You'll find that the extra length the atlatl adds to your arm gives you extra throwing power.

Army footwear

▼ As an ordinary soldier you'll go bare-foot. But if you're promoted to officer rank you'll wear *cactli* – ankle-strap sandals of animal hide or plaited cactus fibre. Top warriors wear sandals with elaborate lacing up to the knees.

13

Have you had your hair cut?

The Aztecs have no army. All men have to do their duty and fight. So, any day, you may have to fight in your first battle. It will be scary, but a chance to show your fighting skills and prove you are a man. Until an Aztec takes his first prisoners, he cannot cut his hair. He's teased by other young men – and by the local girls.

The fate of prisoners

▼ Prisoners are sacrificed in many different ways. Sometimes they are given weapons made of feathers and forced to fight fully-armed warriors. The blood they shed before they die is food for the gods.

Battle tactics

▲ Aztec battles are loud and extremely violent. At the start warriors shout, blow bone whistles and make fearsome booming noises on conch horns. Then archers and javelin-throwers rush forward to attack. Then come soldiers, with spears and swords, advancing side by side in close formation.

Taking prisoners

Special troops with ropes follow the Aztec swordsmen into battle. Their task is to tie up the captives and take them away.

Young man's god

▼ Xochipilli is young man's god. He brings love, music, and dancing. He is honoured by Aztec soldiers, along with the warrior-god Huitzilopochtli and Mictlantecuhtli, god of the dead.

A statue of the god Xochipilli

Close combat

▲ When Aztec troops get close to their enemies they start fighting differently. They stop trying to kill the enemy soldiers, or make them run away in terror. Instead, they do their best to capture them alive. Each Aztec swordsman fights hand-to-hand with a single enemy, hoping to overpower him.

Will you miss home cooking?

All Aztecs know what it's like to go hungry. In years without rain you've seen maize shrivel in the fields and garden vegetables wilt and die. You've gone hunting for any food you can find – wild sage seeds, snakes, deer, cactus fruit and lakeside algae. Now, when you march off with the army, get ready to use those survival skills. You'll have to live off the country! It's a long way between towns with markets and warehouses of stored grain.

Feeding the family

▶ Your mother spends hours every day cooking and serving food. It's hard work crushing dry maize kernels on a *metlatl*. Tortillas are your basic food. They are made from crushed maize and lime-water. This mixture is kneaded and shaped into thin flat cakes, before being baked on a griddle over fire.

▼ Leaving home for war will not be easy. You'll miss your family! You love them and, as a man, you've got used to them looking after you. Your wife and mother feed you, comfort you and make your clothes. Your little sisters help them – and tease you!

This is really good!

Other food

Catch fish with traps, spears or nets. You can net turtles and frogs, too.

Aztecs think that lizards, fish eggs and agave-cactus worms all taste delicious.

All-American

▶ The Aztecs eat many plants and animals that at this time (around AD 1500) are found nowhere else on earth.

maize

sweet potatoes

tomatoes

peppers

turkey

armadillo

tapir

I hope you'll get enough to eat when you're away fighting.

Pottery griddle

Cooking methods

▼ Aztecs have no iron or steel, so your mother uses utensils of pottery or stone and an oven of sun-baked clay. She'll light a fire inside, rake out the ashes, then stew food in pots in the embers.

clay oven   *pottery grater (rough inside)*   *serving bowl*

Warrior feast

◀ Women serve *pulque* (cactus beer) to feasting guests. As a warrior, you'll share in many celebrations. The most important is 'the great feast of the lords', held during the first seven days of the eighth month (June-July). Then, the emperor provides food and drink, and soldiers sing and dance all night long.

Will you be able to travel?

Y ou're lucky! The Aztec empire stretches from the Pacific Ocean to the Gulf of Mexico. You might live anywhere in this vast territory with an army garrison controlling conquered land. You might march to defend the frontier, or hurry to nearby Tlaxcala – where the Aztecs are always at war. You'll see fine sights and meet new people. But travelling means walking, because the Aztecs go almost everywhere on foot!

A fine capital city

▼ Tenochtitlán, capital of the Aztec empire, is a magnificent city. Over half a million people live there. Huge temples surround its central square.

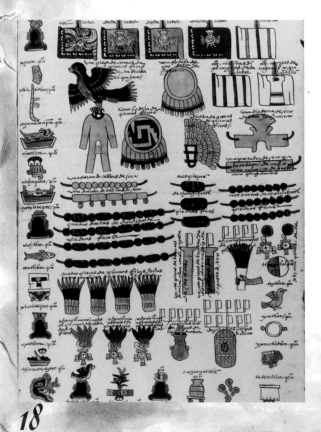

Riches for the emperor

◄ This page from a splendid codex (Codex Menoza) shows why the Aztec empire is so rich. It lists all the valuable tribute (forced gifts) which the emperor demands (and gets) from conquered territory – and from cities that wish to stay free of Aztec control. They send huge quantities of valuable produce to the Aztec capital. The emperor keeps some and sells the rest.

18

Roads and communications

▶ There are roads linking conquered cities throughout the Aztec empire, but no horses or wheeled transport. Urgent messages are carried in forked sticks by fast runners. Porters carry heavy loads.

Messengers, merchants, spies

The Aztecs won their empire by fighting and the emperor still uses the threat of war to conquer more land. First he sends messengers to ask the rulers of rich cities to submit to Aztec rule. But if they do not agree he orders his army to attack. Emperors also send *pochteca* (merchants) to cities they want to conquer. The merchants act as spies, observing, remembering and reporting all they have seen.

To expand the empire even more, past Aztec emperors made a 'Triple Alliance' with two other powerful Mexican cities – Texcoco and Tlacopan.

Buying and selling

▼ Tlatelolco is a great market city, now part of Tenochtitlán. You reach it by canoe or a causeway. Tribute goods, craftwork and food are sold there. Aztecs have no coins, so trade by barter (exchange) or use cacao beans and quills filled with gold dust.

Tribute goods

cloak

warrior's uniform

feather shield

basket of chillies

◀ These *glyphs* (picture-symbols) copied from a codex, show some of the tribute goods sent to the Aztec emperor.

Could you eat a captive?

Like other Aztecs, you believe the world is ruled by nature-gods. They control the weather, the seasons, and time itself. They have destroyed and recreated the world four times already. This is the fifth and final creation. If the gods destroy the world again it will be gone forever. So you must please them with festivals and sacrifices!

Measuring time

▼ The Sun Stone shows the four world ages (labelled) that were created and destroyed by the gods. Aztecs honour over sixty gods; all are different views of one supreme power. The face of the Sun stares out from the centre of the stone.

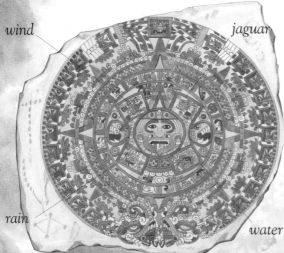

wind

jaguar

rain

water

New Fire Ceremony

▲ The Aztecs use two different calendars: the holy calendar for priests and scribes, and the farmers' calendar for everyone else. Every 52 years both end at the same time. Aztecs fear the world will end too. They put out all fires and wait, full of fear, in the dark. When the stars appear, they sacrifice a man, and light a new fire in his chest.

20

Temple fire

▶ Sticks from the burning sacrifice are used to light a New Fire in the temple, and then the New Fire is taken on lighted sticks to all homes in Aztec lands.

Human sacrifices

◀ This stone container shaped like an eagle holds hearts from human sacrifices.

Feeding the gods

Aztec people see how the earth-gods provide food plants, and the sky-gods send life-giving rain. They know that without these 'gifts' they would die. They believe they must feed the gods in return, to show their thanks. So they give them human flesh and blood.

A prisoner to sacrifice

▶ If you capture prisoners in battle, they will be taken to temples for sacrifice by the priests. Their hearts will be cut out – and you will get some of their flesh to eat as a holy meal.

Are there many dangers?

You've seen enemy captives suffer horribly – as sacrifices and as slaves. So you must expect your own life as a warrior to be full of pain from battle-injuries. You may also suffer from fevers, ulcers, boils and intestinal worms. All are part of daily life. Few Aztecs live for much longer than 40 years. How long will you manage to stay alive?

A doctor's remedies

▼ A *ticitl* (Aztec doctor) offers many different treatments. In battle, he'll bandage your wounds. Back home, he'll try herbal medicine, steam baths, divination or magic spells.

> I can see into the future. You'll soon be dead.

How to stay well

▶ You hope the gods can heal you. But you fear that they might send disease if you offend them or break their religious rules, so try not to.

Faith healing

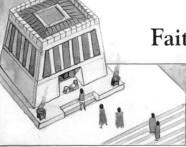

Go to a temple and let priests sprinkle you with holy water.

Make offerings of food to the gods, or kneel and say prayers.

Healing herbs

▼ Ticitls use over 1200 medicinal plants. Some of them are very poisonous. If you die, Aztecs say it is the will of the gods.

Ant

► Try to avoid the snakes and other poisonous creatures.

Scorpion

Spider

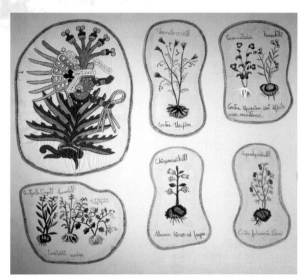

A page from a 16th-century book of herbal medicine

Magic and mystery

◄ Aztecs also believe that enemies can send magic weapons to harm you, and that evil spirits and wandering ghosts can kill. Doctors may give you mind-altering drugs made from plants. They claim this will let your brain make contact with the spirit world, so you can find out what is making you ill.

morning glory

tobacco

peyote fungus

psycobilin mushrooms

Steam bath

► Ticitls also use steam baths to cure such illnesses as aching joints and colds. Patients sit in a mud-brick room filled with steam from the wood-burning furnace next door. They get very hot and sweat a lot, hoping that this will cure them by driving out the illness.

23

What rank will you be?

When an Aztec boy is born, the midwife buries his umbilical cord with tiny arrows and a shield, and tells him that his destiny is to fight. How well will you serve as a warrior? If you capture or kill four enemies, you can become an officer. You'll wear a feather headdress and take part in councils of war. After this you could be promoted to be a commander. But unless you are nobly born, you'll never be an eagle or jaguar knight.

Jaguar knights

▶ Jaguar knights are one of the two highest army ranks. They wear jaguar skins and dedicate themselves to the warrior god Tezcatlipoca. To the Aztecs jaguars are symbols of the underworld – and of silent strength and cunning.

Other careers for boys

▲ Strong and clever, but no good at fighting? Then become a government official.

▲ Prefer to be a priest? You can still fight. Some warrior priests have a career in the army.

24

► Stone portrait of an eagle warrior. He wears a feather-trimmed wooden helmet shaped like an eagle's head.

Eagle knights

▲ Eagle knights are the other top rank in the army. They train at a special college close to the great temple in the centre of Tenochtitlán. They learn to be brave and withstand pain by making sacrifices of their own blood. In battle their duty is to risk their lives by leading the fighting. To the Aztecs, their eagle uniform represents the sun shining brightly at dawn – a sign of new life, hope and strength.

A deadly knife

▼ Sharp stone knife used to kill captives as sacrifices. On its handle is the carved figure of a crouching eagle knight.

Could you land the top job?

The first Aztec emperor came to power by fighting. But now even the best warriors are unlikely to rule. For over 100 years emperors have come from the same royal family. When an old emperor dies, nobles, army commanders, retired senior soldiers, priests and calpulli leaders all meet to choose one of his sons or grandsons to be the new ruler. Unless you've got royal blood, there's not much chance that you'll get the top job!

▼ The emperor is head of the council of nobles and officials that runs the Aztec government. It's his duty to lead discussions of new plans.

▼ After an emperor is chosen, he makes sacrifices to the gods, then puts on splendid robes and goes out to meet the people.

The 'four great ones'

In wartime the emperor is helped by noble officers known as 'the four great ones'. It is their duty to command divisions of the army and organise weapons' supplies. Usually they are members of the royal family but, if you are a truly exceptional soldier, the emperor might make you a 'great one'.

▼ Emperors travel in litters (portable beds) carried by nobles. As a sign of respect, their feet must not touch the ground.

Headdress

Royal clothing

▲ Emperors wear special clothes to show their rank. Only they wear the _xicolli_ (decorated waistcoat). When they serve as priests, in rituals representing gods, they wear magnificent headdresses of gold and quetzal feathers.

An emperor's duties

◄ The Aztec emperor has many duties. The most important are to guide the government and lead his people in war. He must also make sure that all citizens have enough food and water, build roads, protect temples and conquer new lands. He leads discussions with neighbouring rulers, controls trade and farming, and upholds the law. He takes part in religious rituals, praying and making offerings on behalf of all Aztecs.

Aztec rulers

► Aztec rulers from (top left) Acamapichtli (1376-95) to Cuauhtemoc (1520-25) the last Aztec ruler (bottom far right).

Acamapichtli (1376-1395) _Huitzilihuitl (1396-1417)_ _Chimalpopoca (1417-1426)_ _Itzcoatl (1427-1440)_ _Moctezuma (1440-1469)_ _Axayacatl (1469-1481)_

Tizoc (1481-1486) _Ahuitzotl (1486-1502)_ _Moctezuma II (1502-1520)_ _Hernan Cortes_ _Cuitlahuac (1520)_ _Cuauhtemoc (1520-1525)_

Long-term prospects

The Aztecs believe that the gods have already decided the future. So what lies ahead for you? Will you die a glorious death in battle? Will you be captured, and possibly sacrificed, by the Aztecs' enemies? Or perhaps you'll live long enough to fight against European invaders? They will arrive in Mexico very soon, and be welcomed by the emperor. But within two years they will defeat the Aztecs' armies and destroy their empire for ever.

One kind of afterlife

▼ If you're killed in peacetime, you'll travel to the underworld to live with Mictlantecuhtli, god of the dead. It's a long, painful journey that takes four years. When you arrive, you'll die again – this time for ever.

▼ The Europeans will have guns – unknown in Aztec lands until the Spaniards invade.

A warrior's fate

If you die fighting bravely, or as a human sacrifice, you'll face a much happier afterlife. You'll spend your days in the sky with other dead warriors, singing and fighting mock battles as a 'companion of the sun'. After four years you'll be reborn as a hummingbird or a butterfly.

Outgunned by Europeans

▼ Aztec warriors with their traditional weapons will be powerless against European guns. They will ask Huitzilopochtli, their national god, for protection, but nothing can help them.

The end of the empire

▲ In 1519 Spanish soldiers, led by Hernan Cortes, will arrive in Mexico seeking gold. The Aztecs will welcome them, believing they represent an ancient priest-king, Quetzalcoatl. But Cortes and his troops will defeat the Aztecs, kill the emperor, and take control of Aztec lands. In 1535, they will make Mexico a colony of Spain, and Spanish settlers will arrive to live and rule there.

An Aztec's burial

▶ This codex picture shows a young man's body ready for burial and wrapped as a mummy-bundle (left). Beside him is food (beans and maize dumplings) for his journey to the underworld.

Your Interview

Answer these questions to test your knowledge, then look at page 32 to find out if you have what it takes to get the job.

Q1 What do ordinary Aztec soldiers wear on their feet?
A Boots
B Sandals
C Nothing at all

Q2 What are glyphs?
A Monsters
B Picture-symbols, used in writing
C Wild animals, hunted for food

Q3 Who sends tribute to Tenochtitlán?
A The Aztecs' friends
B The Aztecs' enemies
C Cities conquered by the Aztecs

Q4 How does the emperor reward brave soldiers?
A By giving them coloured cloaks
B By giving them land
C By paying them money

Q5 What is the punishment for getting drunk in public?
A Death
B A fine
C A warning

Q6 Who is snake-woman?
A The deputy emperor
B A witch
C Your wife, when she's angry with you

Q7 What are dead warriors reborn as?
A Gods
B Hummingbirds and butterflies
C Eagles and jaguars

Q8 Who fights with feather swords?
A Children
B Magic birds
C Captives being sacrificed

Q9 How many calendars do the Aztecs' priests have?
A One
B Three
C Twenty

Q10 What are Aztec swords made of?
A Iron
B Gold
C Wood and obsidian

Glossary

Agave Cactus with long pointed fleshy leaves.

Ancestor Relative who died long ago.

Atlatl Wooden spear-thrower. It acted as an extension of the arm, so spears could be thrown with greater force.

Barter Exchanging goods for others of equal value.

Cacao Tree that produces beans from which chocolate is made.

Cactli Sandals of animal hide or plaited cactus fibre.

Calpulli Family or neighbourhood group that owned land, provided education and kept law and order.

Conch-shell Large, horn-shaped shell of a sea-creature.

Dart Small sharp spike.

Emblems Designs or symbols that give a message, and are easy to recognise.

Glyph Picture symbol used in Aztec writing.

Granary Building for storing grain.

Javelin Small light spear.

Litter Portable bed.

Mesoamerica Middle part of the American continent, from central Mexico in the north to Nicaragua in the south.

Metalatl Curved stone for grinding grain.

Mummy-bundle Body arranged in a sitting position and wrapped in layers of cloth before being buried.

Obsidian Black glassy stone, produced when volcanoes erupt.

Pochteca Aztec travelling merchants.

Quetzal Rainforest bird with beautiful green feathers.

Quill A feather's hollow central 'spine'.

Sacrifice Killing people or animals as gifts for the gods.

Scorpion Creature related to a spider, with a poisonous sting in the tail.

Ticitl Aztec doctor.

Tlatoani Name of the Aztecs' emperor.

Tortillas Thin crisp maize pancakes.

Tribute Taxes conquered peoples pay.

Umbilical cord Tubes carrying blood from a mother to her unborn baby.

Wild sage Plant with tiny edible seeds.

Xicolli Decorated waistcoat worn only by the emperor.

Index

Have you got the job?

Count up your correct answers (below right) and find out if you got the job as an Aztec warrior.

Your score:

8 Congratulations! It's your destiny.
7 Nearly ready. Keep on training with your calpulli.
5-6 Promising. You'll never make an eagle knight, though.

3-4 Not so good. Perhaps you should be a scribe, or priest.
3 or less Perhaps you're fated for poverty.

Q1 (C) page 13
Q2 (B) page 11
Q3 (C) page 18
Q4 (A) page 9
Q5 (A) page 9
Q6 (A) page 7
Q7 (B) page 28
Q8 (C) page 14
Q9 (B) page 20
Q10 (C) page 12